Blue Heart

A COLLECTION OF POETRY

By Ema Shortel

Blue Heart
by Ema Shortel

Copyright © 2019 Ema Shortel

Little you

little you,
the kitchen floor feels cold on your bare feet and you just want some water
mum shouts at you but she doesn't mean it
she is just tired
it's all going to be ok

you are the lucky one

he adores you
& she is a gentle voice in the chaos
there is much to learn little one

try your best not to be afraid of the loud voices
they are just a cry out for help
you can't do much right now

but you will
just remember there is so much beauty yet to come
Little you

I painted you something today
pretty colours but the rain washed it away
I'd like you to hold me until the sun sets
under a blanket
I wonder if the sky has regrets

pulling at the loose threat on my dress
you tell me to "stop that"
no amount of sleep can ease this restless

light it up just to watch it burn
"soon" you say

soon it will be my turn

- *light it up*

I jump from hope to hope

as if my heart can keep up
as if it won't fall and tumble from its cage

feeling betrayed but free

with the trees so green & the buildings so tall
I can never quite land on my feet

and with all that clutter in your painted windows
how do you let spring in?

I've long since felt the rays of gold upon my ivory skin
the feeling of deep red cherry's that are sure to blossom
from my lips

although,

I jumped once again
landing somewhere new
and the trees are bare, the earth damp

the promise of colour is all I need

- hopes & dreams

Telling tales

moments became minutes, that became hours
as the moon tilted to the right
the hours fell, like sand
turning into years
impossible to catch with eager hands

years squeezed themselves into decades
as you feverishly wonder where you left
that little girl who dreamt of one day

when one day is today
and then even that becomes yesterday

days, months, years unknowingly leaving
the bitter taste of regret on your hungry lips

all the while the world spins and spins

telling tales
of how the flowers bloom from the earth and not from you

32 Portland St

number 32 on a street still there
two flights of stairs & two gardens
a tree built for spring
pretty and purple

a room sighed in whispers of giggles
echoing to the cupboard
and there underneath the stairs
we locked up our dreams
& make believe was the crack in the window

take me back to when we were smaller than the giant's
and taller than the ants
when the sun sunk into the warm concrete

always too soon

leaving behind a glow
we'll never feel again

the sun sets on my youth
"don't cry, you're a big girl now"
but big girls do cry
and it hurts more now than ever

    - cry like me

she bites her lip
the bottom one
when she is anxious
about mundane things

the noise of her tired mind
shatters and cracks
and I hear it
every star freckled night
when the bathroom taps drips
the pipes groan and moan
but she sleeps
and I can't help but peek
into the blood red of her deepest nightmares

- *mother*

one night when things got dark
I found a little alien in my wall
in amongst the brick and paint
feasting on moonlight
rested & alone

he was not big
he was not small
but rather no size at all
and he did not understand why I was crying
or why I was upset at anything in this big, beautiful world

he saw with little knowing eyes that were not there
& he knew of worlds not yet found
he told me of suns that did not burn
and he offered comfort when days took my breath away with heavy
punches

this little alien in my wall
he cared about nothing of silly fears
yet he was everything to me
no form and no thoughts
just his being and all knowing
and after a little while
when the drapes opened to blinding light
he faded away into dust
that floated and danced on the bright thin air

once he was there and now gone
this little alien I missed
although I knew he was with me
day after day
guiding me
and I just had to close my eyes
to feel that it was me

it was me all along

- *intuition*

here in my secret garden
decorated in emerald green
endless flowers
magical colours never before seen

here in my secret garden
who is it that sings?
it's the voices in the wind
they whisper secret things

here in my secret garden
all is not what it seems
searching for the lost
can we look inside your dreams?

here in my secret garden
mind your step, don't trip, don't fall
the ground is as dark and deep
as the trees are tall

here in my secret garden
hush now don't make a sound
silently we'll keep looking
but the secret is

we never wish to be found

- *secret garden*

A.B.C —·

you spoke of coffin nails
& how they killed
eternally cool
white t- shirt, Levi jeans
speckled paint
a shock of colour

you spoke of the little bird
who flew away
poems of different times
voices of a life that hurt
abandoned but not lost

you spoke of giants and manners
hands that took on the world

"follow your heart
reach for the sky
you can do it"

but then you were gone
without warning

they spoke of how you were big & strong
I knew your heart was made from feathers
I whisper to the bird that flew back to me
after the heaviness of that day

now I speak of you with stones in my heart
& spring showers stirring my memories
I speak of how you've never left me

not really

he taught her of the kindness
that rests within
deep in the corners of each & every one of us
and how to sing it to the surface
on the days it would be the only hero

because kindness is a gift
you can & must deliver to yourself
the only kindness we can control

bathe yourself in this day & night
pores full of softness and honey

and my darling girl
this is how you shine
this is how you forgive yourself

- *lesson no.1*

you were told to keep wishing
although

they disappeared in between your teeth
seeping into wet hair and heavy clothes

and all at once you can't seem to remember
the green of hope
the pink of rose petals
& the frost of your perfect morning

stick out your tongue & hope, hope
that your wishes melt
before
the world breaths you in again

  - perfect morning

Built from pain —⋖

you hold onto these building blocks of life
still that little girl inside
who liked to run
and who looked up

always up

at the people & the wonder
and the sheer height of it all

"oh how big we wish to be"

we're all just wanderers
we put one foot in front of the other
and it leads us to a series of moments
we hope that the next one will be better

always better

but what if it's the seconds in between the steps that count?
like turning the kitchen light off (I took a breath)
or inhaling your warmth
or when you tell me I am nice & good
or when we stare out at the rain & smile at strangers

what if we're looking for bigger moment's
all the while missing
the light that waits in the silence

- silence

maybe I decided to dance
maybe I went to school, learnt new things
made new friends
maybe I was good
maybe I got a lucky break & left here
maybe I liked it
maybe I was beautiful
maybe I flourished
& maybe people loved me
maybe I missed home sometimes
but life was too exciting to come back
maybe I had a different story to tell
maybe I spoke to myself softer
& fed my body the right things
maybe I smiled more in the mirror
maybe if I had stuck around

I could have had a life I was proud of

- *my story*

what a noisy world we live in
heaviness falling in step as our shadows
always bigger than the young soul within

what a cruel way to be
stripped of childish eyes
self -loathing carved into your smooth back
addicted to ugly lies

and day by day our lungs give in
threatening to stop at once
with the smoke & the glass
murmuring into the bright new day
reflecting what you should become

you called for a break
for a heart that does not bleed in gallons
when the dew sets in & the moisture sparkles
give this body a rest

here upon this earth with the quiet forest
or the roaring of the ocean
the noise that does not try to drown us out
but instead
caresses the very essence of these atoms

- what should I become?

You don't look happy —

my dear girl,

what do you see?
what emotions haunt your gaze?
what burdens your colourful mind?
what beauty haunts you so?

they'll tell you to drink up

"smile"

don't let them know you are upset
don't let your hair fall out of place
is your skin just right?
were you polite enough?
good enough?
they'll tell you to eat that
don't be wasteful

"smile"

have confidence
change your hair
let it down this time
it's not ladylike to act this way
they'll tell you to like this, like that

"smile"

did you do enough today?
change the world today?
and suddenly, I can't breathe

"smile"

move they'll say
but I can't
and I don't think I can smile
not today

Part 2

Here's to learning where this *pain* comes from

Bad habits —◄

bad habits

swimming in the velvet sky
following trails of kindness
shaking you from comfort to whisper secret things
catching lines of silver as it melts from your fingertips

obsessing over old moons

wearing constellations of you in my hair
smiling with sad eyes

bad habits
bad habits
bad habits

how tiring it is to think
fear sewn into tiny cracks around your eyes
& your smile
this day is made up of things not soft
no matter how many times the sun sets me alight
I am yet to turn my back on ice

- fire & ice

I can't help but take big juicy bites out of life
happiness drips from my fingertips
sticky
and it drips from my hair & the end of my nose
but when the bite is sour
and sometimes it is
the drips become a rainstorm

my teeth begin to rot
mouth full of regret

take a glass of water and drink it down

"my dear slow down
sip once in a while
life was not made to swallow whole"

but the sun brings around more ripe fruit
& I don't even want to stop myself
not even one little bit

it may be a touch of pain covered in sugar
yet I bite down as if I had nothing else
in the universe to do

- hindsight

the hell to my hello
and I said I wouldn't
yet here I stay
goose bumps & wet skin
with just enough breath to say

"do it again"

- infatuation

eyes closed, chest forward
hands behind my back
and then I fall
like I have a million times before
leaving only the moon behind
to sigh once more
at my willingness
to apologise
for the way I fell for you

- open your eyes

Slaughterhouse —

I want to pull the world up over my head
hang this meat & skin on the hanger
after this long day
maybe I can scrub the shame from my skeleton
dispose of all the noise & ugly we do

maybe then I can rest
maybe then I can begin to forgive
all of what we have caused

there is a rot in my brain
a love that is lost
there is soil in my heart
heavy & black

no flowers bloom here

your fingernails are dirty
your feet damp
and I can't breathe under this weight

you toy with me
knowing the beauty of our colours
still you feed that rot
& starve that soil

- Rot

I hate myself in the light
I hate my hands and how they stay
I hate myself in the dark
I hate myself dangled in chains of daisy's
I hate my skin after the whip of your breath
I hate myself under their gaze
I hate my lips & how they shake
I hate myself in the light
I hate myself despite

- self -loathing

the pain was everything
it was the sky above
it was the kind looks
& the pitying stares
it was my numb fingers buttoning up my shirt
& it was the shade of red on my lips

everything

it was the day's trickling by
in blurry waves of discomfort
it was a gaping hole in my chest
& it was the 6am news

it was the changing of the seasons
the rain that threatened
& the murmur of conversation

it was the sharp blade that cut my snow -white skin
& it was the warmth that came in floods

& now the pain belongs to all these things
& not to me

- *stop the world, I need to get off*

Technicolour nightmares

what a fool for asking
for black & white daydreams
when all you wrote
were technicolour nightmares
I yearned for a splash of colour
& you drowned me
here in rainbows of death

how beautiful to watch
the failings of a soul so pure
trusting & true
although not always innocent
in the ways we had hoped

what a dangerous dream
ivory fingers playing to me
melting from fibres & solar systems
until I am but the bittersweet memory
of you
of me
of us & what was

what a fool
a silly little fool

I tripped over the truth of you
crawling over raised voices & bruised knuckles
falling when I can
you offer a hand when you remember
the softness of my shell cracks & falters
under your bursts of lightning

then out of the corners of your smile
warmth trickles down your spine
& I can't help but stop & stare
at the rainbows my soft & your storm
will forever paint

- *sticky truth*

she runs head- first into the colours of you
if you looked, you'd realise the beauty of it

- collision

Cells of you

why must you let him make up
the cells of you?

the lights, the smiles
those are mine
the air in your air & the flush on her cheeks
although as I see the whole picture
I see I am not there
& the promises that were made
are just echoes of the past

dreams of poems & marked skin
to have a friend by my side
is all I wanted

one step, one hope after another
thrown over the edge
ripped paper & jumbled words
falling to the sea
I wait for the certainty of the tide
whilst I taste the wet on my lips

but her smile is not mine
& the flush on her cheeks is not mine

- matching tattoos

your face sticky from the journey
cheeks red
palms sweaty
you ask for it & I let you drink from me
I've held this perfectly wrapped box for too long
rip me open with your teeth
smudging me
getting dirt underneath your fingernails
scratching away the ice -cold grip on my neck
stimulating the fantasy that tiptoes
around my dainty wrists
pinholes of yellow light
little & then a lot
a smile cracks & the world is upside down
history will tell you
of how I hid my happiness in you

- *history*

his eyes are softer when I look pretty
as if he is relieved in my beauty

- *beauty hurts*

Even souls can bruise —

with all you knew
of me & my hair full of moonlight
the mud still stained the carpet & the fireplace rug
embers set uncertainty up in flames
whispers on your neck
little hairs made up of imperfect

squelch, squelch
with my tenderness in your hands

even souls can bruise

life passes by drip by drip
trapped with no lungs
in this body of mine
why do I hate me so much?
why does it hurt?
I cry & I cry
alone & a little sad
my hands over this face
soft & ugly
a little voice inside
tells me lies & I don't like it
so how can I break free from this dark?
it's so very dark
& my ribs are bound to break
under the pressure of my self- loathing
I plead with myself
snap out of it, dear child
before you crumble & fall

- an almost soul

gentle does it with this heart of mine
tiptoe & whisper
we look both ways
frightened with collections of wounds
listening to the echoes of our breaks

but if you are lucky enough
you'll creep up on me when I am distracted
when I am looking up
you can peek into my chest now
view galaxies of love & planets that orbit my wild soul
please keep me safe
no sudden moves
make me trust
for too many have toyed with this gentle body
ran their feather fingers up my spine
only to reach inside & tear me apart
inch by inch relentlessly
not satisfied until they find their own stars
through my skin & bone

there's enough here for you
I would have handed over my whole world
sun & moon & all
no need to pour me out
taking for yourself
so please, gentle does it with this heart of mine

- I said NO

the sky feels heavy tonight
like a suffocating argument
closing in
I want to scream
but I am unable to find my voice
in the fog that's filling my lungs
I want you to tell me I am pretty
but all you do is stare
at the ugly parts of today
caught in my hair & pooling at my feet

I'd run but I can't
I'd cry but I can't
I'd feel sad but I can't

tomorrow
perhaps I'll feel better under a new sky
perhaps you'll tell me I'm pretty, then

- stop staring

Crying in bathrooms

you ate too much sugar
and you're sure to regret it
your heart raced as you said hello
to the strangers in the bar
you worried your imperfect skin could be seen
under the harsh lights
you wanted to say something
but you were shy & stayed quiet instead
the music felt funny
dancing tightly between your ribs
uncomfortable breath
coming in short bursts
you were hungry again
you just wanted to sleep
you were tired
always tired
and they laughed at something you didn't quite catch
you smiled anyway
ease in the way they moved & spoke
you ached for that freedom
you stayed in that cage all night long
only letting go when you quietly excused yourself
and you wept silent in the bathroom
and you listed in painful lines along your tender thighs all the things that
are wrong with you

but my eyes are tired & my bones are tired
and my fingernails can't scratch
my legs are tired
and my smile is tired
and the floorboards crack
with laughter lines
maybe if I lie down
I won't be so tired

maybe

maybe the floor will tell me it's ok to scratch
but my eyes are still tired & my bones are still tired

- *tired still*

that feeling
suffocating in a rainbow
sipping on his lies as the world leaves you behind
eating the crumbs of your ok's
a tight smile lingers & you're crying in the bathroom
can I rest my head on your chest?
goose bumps from your breath & then sleep

oh, what a feeling

- lie to me

I'm ok —·⋘

a whisper of an ache
a slow painful sob
a sticky rainstorm in your lungs
a smile swallowed whole by the battering of dialogue
a sweaty heartbeat throbbing in your ears
a war inside your bones
crunching, breaking, screaming
& it's always the way
behind emerald green eyes
behind the lump you can't push down
behind the breath you almost forgot to take
behind the noise that comes thrashing in waves

a pause
"I'm ok"

this is for you
for you & your little box of emotions
this is from me with my seasons of love

my winter froze your hands in place
at your side with a muted voice
but I've seen the fire & I seen a friend
our bodies ached with summer melting
frostbite from our hearts
I looked at you from the bright side of the sun
the warm showers raced down your back

still I could not keep up
running through lighter nights & red lights
overtaking your fears & doubts
and yet summer turned on itself once again
as did you
with new moons & new shelter
undercover from my seasons

this is for you
this is from me

- seasons of love

my screams caught fire as they kissed the air
with silence teasing your lips
all you could do was stop and stare
I turned my back & walked away
oh silence, beg me
beg me to stay
wet eyed & white knuckled
still no sound reached my ears
now I taste the rain
I taste it in my tears

- I would have stayed

sadness
it tosses & turns, gripping, ripping through my veins
tearing time apart
silently suffocating
you are the stars that burst from my chest
yearning to live
I am just a re-lived kindness, here to keep the flames
warm in my hands
tender & teary eyed

- sadness

Violent dance

watching this violent dance
with her sharp red heels
& his threatening stare
neither side lost of a tentative touch

a perfect symphony of explosions
an audience mesmerised by the quick steps
bodies synchronised avoiding licks of flames

cuts from the fallen stars
they stay in this dream like state
exhausted but beautiful

faster & faster they sway to the melody of time
numbers & words fall from her dress
memories caught in his curls

oh
how dangerously addictive this violent dance can be

I was sad in the morning
sunlight & hurt tracing my skin
your lips lingered
leaving stains of passion all over my face
why would you not smile with your eyes?
all I needed was a spark of hope
words failed & you were gone

- nothing left to say

lOvE...
what a tricky little thing
showing breathe taking sunsets
tricking you to the dark side of the moon
head in your hands after the night bites

your chest a jagged thing
bearing sharp teeth when needed
only to reveal the redness of your heart
a beautiful living murmur of a song I sing to you
my cut hands dripping more than yours
puddles on the wooden floor
& your childish grin spreads at the sight of me
this isn't a game
this tricky thing we call love
but if it was

you would win

- check mate

Haunted from my skin

the snow falls as if it had forever to land
warmth a thing of the past
there is a hint of a glow
just around the corner of my mind
a memory of kinder looks
and intertwined hands
but 2am aches for 9am
where the burn melts away the silence
that rests in these walls
here in my body you'll find a home
paint the walls red & close the windows

I've seen enough of this blue world
the beauty of you haunts me from my skin
& just like that I am gone
& you live on

disturbingly tired in a town that does not sleep
run down with black smoke
dancing in my limp hair
stained white teeth with coffee in your veins
"can I have another cigarette please?"
dark eyes and polished lips
prepared for retaliation
daisy's in my crown
no thorns here
yet if I were to ponder twice
I may have chosen roses
the yellow kind

the grass needs cut but no one looks
another day goes by
exchanging inches for time
happiness for laughter lines

I may have met a boy, but it slips my mind
he liked red but I can't recall how I knew
& the gentle in his eyes was a place I called home
his name I did not know

this tired town is all I see from here on out
still, I wait for the boy, but he does not come by too often
my daisies have turned grey
and I seemed to slip away
to where the sun was not the sun
& the stars were not the stars
but rather the boy with the gentle eyes
& I can recall it all now
the beauty in the cosmos
if only a little too late

- the ghost of me

These are the problems —

these are the problems
trinkets of broken bone
just as your sun bathes his skin
rays of honey dripping from your chin
oh, if he could see
for decades he would weep

but me
I fall & breath him home
that's where we'll perish
dark eyes & new stars

these are the problems

put the phone down
you still have a couple hours left to sleep

"my eyes sting"

you left this morning in a rush
I missed you instantly
I long for a lingering kiss
you slammed a door last night & I can
still hear the echo

these walls don't speak but if they could
would they speak of the cracks growing day by day
or would they speak of how I linger
waiting to be painted
in the colours of your love?

- the morning after

our mess amuses us
avoiding the shirts hanging from the ceiling
you hold my breath in your eyes
I beg
don't blink
we may suffocate
on the sharp edges of this love

- delicate

Unheard wishes   —✒

upon your cheek a small wish fell
do you dream of us? It's hard to tell
no stars above
no path to guide
without your hand I stand by your side
I whispered the world into your ear
the words were too heavy, they were never clear
I held out my secrets for you to hold
maybe tomorrow was all I was told

so up on my toes I reached for the sky
you looked, if only you asked why
it got warm all around and on our backs
chasing the heat, you avoided the cracks
soon you were too far, you strayed
I held the sun right here
I wish you had stayed

a stranger's lungs
rejecting puffs of white across the way
into the night
this night with all its ink coloured promises
does the stranger think as I do?
does she wonder why too?
and with questions dancing through the night breeze
I sigh my last sigh
& I blow out the candle
my own black smoke escaping to meet the stars

- summer nights

Re written

I do not know who I am
a shell, empty
& people feel wrong
leaving fingerprints all over me
smudging, cracking, falling
I just want to be liked
I don't know if that makes me good or bad
& I don't know who has all the answers
maybe there are none
maybe they'll rain on me one day
a surprise shower of hope

until then I am a wanderer of this life
searching for trails of anything
wishing to be full like you
like them

take me back to before I knew
how to feel uncomfortable in my own skin
I guess I'll stay here
tears & broken drawn on my face

waiting to be re written

hold you in my bones
tracing lungs with your fingertips
watching the sand fall
yet time never quivers
a rib cage full of hate
my heart you eat
as sweet as the dawn
a scream bottled up in my dreams
burning up, up, up

but oh, a sigh

bundle me up in the thorns of your touch
softened by the scent of your feather eyelashes
hold you in that treasured smile
bundle me up in the velvet sky of yesterday

- *nostalgia*

Make me a fairy tale —·⋖

but what if I need the fairy tale?
things that will never exist
only in my childish mind
do I see us touching the sky?
only to be burnt by the sun
"yes"
a million times yes
passionate years & bursts of lust
falling from heavy heights
forever ill land in your dizzy playground
lights & sparks flying
blind but we can still feel
feel the fire that led us here
fingertips melting with smiles that spread
across our rosy cheeks, muddy palms
you can make me a fairy tale
dark & light all at once

I wonder do you feel it too
do you tilt your head up when things get quiet?
letting the moon take in your beaten soul
as you tiptoe around everything that hurts
wearing your unspoken words as a crown
are you empty of me?

I wonder

- your crown

Despite it all   —⋅⤝

I'm the girl that cries
when you look away
I'm the girl who can't breathe
but smiles anyway
I'm the girl who straightens her skirt
& brushes her hair
war paint seen for miles & miles

I'm the girl who aches for more
I'm the girl who knows you
I'm the girl who wishes under shooting stars
whispers of what could be
hairs on your neck stand on end
birds fly overhead

I'm the girl who marvels at weeds & the green
I'm the girl who wakes at midnight
laughing at the silliness of it all

I'm the girl who understands it hurts
I'm the girl that bleeds with you
I'm the girl with scars & daggers
I'm the girl with the bottled- up scream
I'm the girl with hidden rage tattooed on her bones

I'm the girl with the gunshot in her heart
I'm the girl who will stand with you
up against it all
I'm the girl who is still here
despite it all

Part 3

Flowers *Bloom* from The Bluest of *Hearts*

We are we   —·⋖

the world is big
gigantic actually
and the sea splits up the middle
electricity slithers and sparks
the veins of this earth

and sometimes we feel like less
less than what, I'm not sure
but one thing I know for sure
is you are you and I am me
and on the days when I feel less
the you-ness of you helps

oh, it helps

when the coffee doesn't kick like it should
or the day holds more weight than health
the clogs get real stuck in my stomach
yet you keep pushing on
through the sludge and the stickiness of it all

and we are we
and that's the one thing I know for damn sure

of all the shades that have ever chosen my skin
of all the colours that have
ran their fingers through my hair
of all the hues
that have kissed me goodnight

you are by far
the brightest

- 2pm rainbows

in a quiet moment
I put my head to your chest
our laughter echoes
in your lungs
our lust
drips through your veins

red wine stains your teeth
a hole in your sock
dirt on your shirt
curls in your hair
and the *heaviness*
of the day in your eyes

this moment holds a thousand long pauses
a million quiet breaths
and a handful of heartfelt words

this moment is the making of you and I
and everything in between

midnight melts from your tongue
and I knew, in that moment
I would never tire
of how it felt on my skin

- *midnight melts*

I love him

I'm never going to give up
I'm going to love him
until it fills him up
until it's pouring out of us
filling up his lungs
swelling my heart
I'll give him every last breath
I will love him until his cheeks hurt
and his hands melt
I will love him until he shines with the stars
and then…

even then I will love him some more

- even then

Heart break hunters —◄

heart break hunters
thrill seekers
dream chasers
the stars align on this stubborn night

for you

clearing a path however small
for your brave, brave soul
fingertips holding onto
the petals of your youth
you pull and you pull
leaving behind moments of magic
within sad eyes
nostalgia seeping into your tired heart

I tell you to "let go"

the slow beat washes over your wild hair
be ready for that glance across a crowded room
because your people are out there
closer than you think
just as impatient as your compass
pointing towards fate
there's only one way to go

so, my fellow dream chaser

walk that path with your head held high
your smile is *beautiful*, I thought you should know

every night
you've ever held yourself together
feeling paper thin
pools of tears dripping from your wings

when the shards of glass sting your feet
and you whispered through gasps

"I need you, I need you, I need you"

yet every night you healed
under the still morning
that always crept upon you
shining on your worn out back
rainbows of electric
leading the way
into a new day
a new hour of hope

and all you could do was hold your bones
high above the pain
and swim towards the shore of broken hearts

feel proud that you made it through
the web of memories
that haunted your lungs

and you shine upon another shadow
and you *heal*

- oh, you heal

pour your broken little heart
into my hands
we'll turn those jagged edges
into a thousand
glistening stars

- 5am

Nicky —·

there are souls that will ask no questions, that will fall into your rhythm day after day. that will hold your hand in the crowds and wipe the hurt from your broken smile. these souls are gentle breezes in a grey world. these souls are the warmth on your face and the flowers in your hair.

these souls are you and I.

my soul sister
my spark
my fighter
my favourite moon

- Jordan

your mind is overwhelming you
your heart is free

- coffee conversations

the melody of life and all its beauty
can you feel it soothing your weary heart?

let it in

let it caress your tired bones
when all is lost
the colourful notes
will lead the way
towards your perfect horizon

- *let it in*

I'd use all my full moon spells for you

- *moon child*

Old moons

on this new day
this new year
I step out reflecting on old moons
I peel this skin
a little torn and a little rough

a chance

to love myself
gently
and fiercely all at once
tracing these scars with pride
here I am
alive and free

oh, so free

I remember being on my own
and I remember feeling sad
I remember the rain
and the sun
sometimes on the same day

I remember the tallness of it all
the suffocating streets and the ferry's

I remember you weren't there
and I remember even when you were
you weren't at all

I remember breaking myself down
and pulling at the corners of my soul
unravelling a colourful mess
quiet and loud all at once

and I remember needing you
but I needed myself more
 and I found those corners
and I built myself from the ground up

- *I remember, I remember*

I slept here
for months and decades
I lay inside myself
tracing oceans and rivers with my fingers
ripples in time

patience, patience

and then out of the corners of my mind
I saw you again
blurry
but you loved another

I got sleepy again
wandering constellations
finding warmth
within any embrace
teeth that nibbled
too scared to really taste me

another trip around the moon
beautiful in all the wrong ways
they said
once more fate blew through my open heart
lightly
but I felt it
and for a second you came into focus
and without hesitation
like a shooting star
my heart aimed for you
heavy and fast
and you caught me, as if I was the miracle you were waiting for

- *miracle*

Irrevocably you —◄

If only you knew
the power that runs through these veins
beaten once again
under a thousand harsh words
yet you see the glint in your heart
the steady hands
and the world tilts
threatening to throw you over
pushing you closer
to the edge
when you thought there was no height
left to fall

that is when you reach inside
to the quiet storm
that causes earthquakes
in your bones
and rainstorms in your eyes

because this is what makes you human
this is what makes you irrevocably *you.*

"we straighten our curls & we chew slowly. we smile politely & dress accordingly. we swallow down arguments, hissing silently into our pillows. we make ourselves pretty for green eyes & greedy hands. we keep love warm in our hands. handing out crumbs for everyone we meet. we make people like us with our sparkly eyes and clever words. we filter the sky and pray under the moon. we forgive all harm & give chances to infinity. we remain soft for your harsh touch. we pull out thorns in the shadows. we cry only in the shower. salt & warmth running down our smooth skin. we think we are ugly but my god we are beautiful. we get together and the magic that hides in veins & heart shine like a thousand lightning strikes all at once. and we are storm and we are one. and they will look up and say we are beautiful"

- the magic of you

I am glad that you are the way you are
and I am glad that I am the way I am
and I am glad that they are the way they are

I am glad that I don't have to wake up
early on a Saturday
I am glad when you wake with a smile
and I am glad when my feet
feel warm under the covers

I am glad when I eat and when I don't
I am glad when I drink and when I am thirsty

I am glad when I am happy and when I am not
I am glad when I make the green light
I am glad when there are pretty pictures to see

I am glad when winter kisses frost
and I am glad when I read

I am glad every day and every night
and even when I am not

I am glad

- glad

but what if I am happy
what if my world spins at a perfect angle?
I pleat the pain at each side of my head
each morning
don't you see?
how shall poems fall from my hair then?

my dear.

they simply don't

when you are high off of all that you are
when you believe in the magic of your sky
and you are drenched in your open smile
you become the poem
and my, it is *spectacular*

- *magic of your sky*

Write you kind

paint me as the leaves you love
the red ones that fall
they're yours
I'm yours
look, really look
like you always said you would
tilt your head with the wind
look pain in the eyes
silently smile
because my love
I have you
and I always will

paint me colourful
and
I'll *write you kind*

I always loved the way she looked
at nothing in particular
and the way she thought of me
as someone she knew
I loved the way her hair
fell down her back
and the way she played with it

endlessly

every day she played
and I loved the way she held me quiet in her heart
nothing big, nothing bold
I loved her silence
and the way she felt like hope
but I think I loved her most of all

not the way

just her

- endlessly her

he tells me he loves me when I need it most
looks me in the eyes
whilst holding me up
my limbs long gone limp
on this horrible day

my friends won't do
they rarely cry like me

and I can't muster enough breath
in my silly little lungs to say it back

but I do

and him knowing when to tell me
the things I need to hear
on the days I yearn for it most
like a match years for its flame

well

it's all I'll ever ask of him

- *ask of him*

they asked me how it felt to love you

I replied

"I love him as if all the stars fell from the sky
and wrapped themselves around me
resting on my collarbone
and my eyelashes
leading a path
towards you
towards me
towards home"

- to love you

Ruby's and gems

I collect your smiles
like a child collects treasure
and as you kiss me gently
on my shivered back
I come to realise
you have gifted me
a chest full of ruby's & gems

and if I could frame all of what I have seen
of this beautiful world
I would find myself
staring at your smile forever

I try on each day
searching for a perfect fit
Monday too heavy
running through to a tight choke
Saturday seems ok, a little loose
but there's no denying
the days that view you
the cracks in the walls heal
and my day fits just right
as if I can't feel the hours at all
just the warmth of your presence
and it all falls away
all the bullshit

and I realise you are my perfect fit

on any day

- perfect fit

morning coffee and the curls in your hair
oh, what a dream
to see me through your eyes
stay in this slumber forever and a day
here is where I'll stay
where promise is given
and the kisses are sweet

- oh, so sweet

Wild snapping

the magic is too fleeting
to worry about straight hair and painted nails
run towards the chaos
with *wild snapping* at your ankles
and freedom shattering your bones

you may think of me as weak
but I know different
you see I've raised this wolf within
all patience and stealth
my understanding my power

and I move, so quiet you won't hear me coming
perfect timing
going in for the kill
always
with elegance

I hunt this life never afraid
never scared of what lurks

and I don't know how you could have ever called me weak
when I saw the blood
dripping from your chin

yet I put my trust in you, anyway

- *trust*

this isn't how I planned it
fast and all at once
all sharp teeth and sweaty nights
but then I wouldn't have it any other way

you see I don't know
if I would enjoy the flames
quite so much from the outside
we burn inside
beautiful and bold
leaving trails of smoke and stardust

and I realise nothing is ever planned
we are simply pushed
gently
by the warm breeze
into the arms of fate

- fate

This is my brave

that which led me to you
 is my *brave* and my favourite part of me

yes, I am soft
I break
into little broken pieces
I shatter as many times as I have to
you'll find me everywhere
all over the carpet
and in between the floorboards

but I am strong
because I am not afraid to let the light in
even when it burns
& it feels uncomfortable on my gentle skin
and you'll find me gasping for air
my body shaking with sobs of pain

as I pick myself up
I ground this body
with wounds that gape
softness is my superpower
with gems that glow blue & calm
hear my voice in the wind

I am *soft*, I am *strong*

- *soft blue*

I walk across, under and around
any path to get to you
this earth with all its salt- water
and green moss
what a magical thing
my bad heart can I start again

and when I reach you beyond forever
& before never
I wish to drown in your smile
I'll paint you from the inside, lighting you up
don't spit me out
let me rest here in your beautiful soul

you see I was built just for you
with feathers in my hair
& sweat upon my skin
an extra set of wings to leave at a moment's notice

always with you my darling

always

- built for you

when your heart breaks like the bones of time
remember you are you
and you can make the night
light up
like a thousand fireflies

- fireflies

From the blue

I fell back
arms out into the silky waves
salt in my hair and bones
hold my heart to your ear
the ocean calls like never before
I'm the girl from the blue
and from the blue

I'll always choose *you*

honey, let go of the edges
dare to peek
take a look
take a look at the bigger picture

because in between the hidden giggles
the spark of an awkward glance
the sweet longing of the unknown
the tug at your lover's sleeve
the sighs and the dried tears on your flush cheeks
we've all felt the ache of a *blue heart*

- *bigger picture*

your mind is a garden dear child
you must tend to the plants
and water the roses

even if it's only tears you have to offer
lick the salt up and realise
oceans taste of your hurt
and we *marvel* at oceans on this earth

- *oceans taste*

Hey you

"hey you"
I know you are working hard
I see you painting over that nasty word they threw at you
you don't have to pretend for me
I've seen all shades of ugly
and I still seek beauty

it's cold and it's dark
and the world spins and spins
without checking to see if you are ok

but you are trying, and you are a *warrior*
and I see you
and you are beautiful

I wish they would dream more
because I am here
waiting amongst the stars
and in between the flowers
resting on a blade of grass
singing in the wind

I leave clues like rain and snow
on your beautiful face
I feel a tug on my sleeve as I close my eyes
the girl with the gold hair
she is ready

I have waited for months or years
I cannot recall
the stars are perfect
on the back of fate
connecting the years
threading the time gone by
in beautiful hues, bright and bold

lightning strikes on a sunny day
although you cannot see
and he crosses your path

if I've ever asked for anything in return
dear child
I ask for you to dream in colour

I'll build rainbows over castles just for you

- law of the universe

be gentle on yourself
the universe craves your brokenly soft soul

- shine bright

Lucky stars

as the sun sneaks its way
slowly under my ungrateful skin
I wonder
of all the moons that have yearned for more silver
instead of thanking
their *lucky stars*

It's an art really —◄

it's an art really

to feel the *rage* of life tear you limb from limb

and yet still find the courage
to smile sweetly in the face of a new day

peel away the imperfect illusion of perfection
throw your little head back and surrender
to those quiet corners of peace
that yearn to be seen

breathe

breathe and see
my darling you are a magical potion
of shining stars
and everything that feels like
smiles and warmth

you are you
and oh, how beautiful that is

- *imperfect*

gratitude my dear
because all of this

it's not a *given*

- *thankful for*

How gorgeous. To be wearing the earth —

some say it needs to hurt to feel real
violence and chaos
painted as a lustful romance

it's ok

but standing here again
with my passionate bruises & ruby red blood
I don't know if I believe
that love shouldn't melt off my bones

beaten into consciousness
I believe love should inhale me
keep me safe inside lungs that breath for once
and I should sleep soundly within dreams of gentle hands
golden hair
smoothed away from my face

a body not afraid to shatter
into a million pieces
because I know you'll pick me up slowly
taking forever to put the puzzle of me
back together

we keep whiskey in this house
smoky & strong
we sigh in this house
when night is long
we scream in this house
vibrations running through our painted windows
we love in this house
hair tangled in throbbing sobs
we keep ourselves in this house
hidden by reality
we look at dreams in this house
laughing at the fools we are
we peek around corners in this house
we run at fears in this house

we keep whiskey in this house

- smoky & strong

you're sitting next to me
we've been at the beach all day
just you and I

God, you are silly

I can taste the salt on your skin
there's laughter lingering in your eyes
my lips are chapped from the wind
you tell me I'm your favourite
you're always saying that

I like it

the blanket feels warm on our shivered bones
when I close my eyes, I still see you
who said that was a bad thing?

you're sitting next to me
and there's nowhere to be
time means nothing but more daylight
to memorise the lines on your face

I sigh and think to myself

my body is tired
my mind is tired
but never of you

"never of you"

End story

Healing is like being found. Being found when you felt like an invisible mess on the floor. But they stop and let you hold their hand and slowly pluck the stars from the sky, one by one to make you believe that magic still exists in this world. And they do something, like smile when you smile, or they make that hand gesture, or their voice sounds just right. It's when you know you can be comfortably quiet with someone and even when your stories fall upon tired ears, they listen, and they will put their cold feet on your legs in the morning.

I'm going to share my morning breath with someone who sparks me on their thigh when I'm all but burnt out. They will bring me back to life and I don't know but to feel like there are people who give just to give & love just to love. That is enough. And it always will be. I know that now. When my photographs end up old memories and my smile leaves traces of sewn in laughter lines you will kiss me, and you will be perfect. And the air will feel neither hot nor cold.

All will feel just as it's aught to.

About the Author

Hi. You made it to the end of my book. That's pretty cool. Thank you for reading. You are officially on my list of favourite people in the world, like EVER.

I never really know what to say when people ask about ME. I suppose I am just a wee Scottish 20 something living in Edinburgh, Scotland and mostly just enjoying my cosy existence. I do not have it all figured out, but I am learning that no one does and that the biggest gift you can give your-self is the freedom of your inner self. You know that wee voice that taps you on the shoulder every now and again when things get quiet? The voice that tells you, you should write that book, take that course, go on that trip, learn that language? Give it the centre stage every once in a while. You never know. There may just be an audience out there aching to hear it.

If you want to connect, you can find me on Instagram under the name
@xoblueheartxo

Come say hey.

Ema Shortel

Printed in Great Britain
by Amazon

33079911R00071